You Have Permission to Succeed

Navigating Your Road to Success

Edwin Haynes

You Have Permission to Succeed: Navigating Your Road to
Success
Copyright © 2010 by Edwin Haynes
E. Haynes Publishing
2470 S. Dairy Ashford, Suite 217
Houston, TX 77077
www.ehaynespublishing.com

Cover design by: Jamaica Johnson
Manuscript edited by: Mignon McCarthy
Printed in the United States of America

Library of Congress Control Number: 2010928763

ISBN 978-0-615-35241-1

"Our deepest fear is not that we are inadequate. Our deepest fear is that we are powerful beyond measure. It is our light, not our darkness that most frightens us. We ask ourselves, who am I to be brilliant, gorgeous, talented, fabulous? Actually, who are you *not* to be? You are a child of God. Your playing small does not serve the world. There is nothing enlightened about shrinking so that other people won't feel insecure around you. We are all meant to shine, as children do. We were born to make manifest the glory of God that is within us. It's not just in some of us; it's in everyone. And as we let our own light shine, we unconsciously give other people permission to do the same. As we are liberated from our own fear, our presence automatically liberates others."

-Marianne Williamson-

ACKNOWLEDGMENTS

Thank God for blessing me with the vision and resources to share my knowledge and experience with the world. I thank Him for the potholes as well as the smooth pavement that has allowed me to successfully reach my destination!

I would like to thank my wife, Andrea, for loving me unconditionally and supporting me on this path to success. With you by my side it has been an awesome journey. I am thankful for the joy of having the blessing of my wonderful children: Destiny, Kaylan and Ashley. I would like to thank my parents, Barbara and Larry Adams, for their constant love and support. Thanks to my brothers and sisters for always supporting me and cheering me on. I would like to extend a special thanks to my dear friend, Holton Buggs, who helped to light a spark under me and guide me on the road to personal growth, development and true financial freedom. I am eternally grateful to all of you for your constant love and support!

CONTENTS

PREFACE

As I traveled up Mount Wuyi and inhaled the clean, crisp air, free from pollution and far from the stress and toils of everyday life, my heart became lighter and full of joy. With each step, the anticipation of reaching the top of this exquisite creation of nature made me feel as if I were floating on air. Once I reached the summit, I took a moment to gather myself and once again inhaled my surroundings. A clean, faint wind swept over me. I smiled and thought of how blessed I was to be standing in this wondrous spot, to have had the opportunity to travel clear across the earth to another world, a world filled with immense possibilities.

I gazed at the faces around me and wondered if they were experiencing the same intense appreciation for life that I was feeling at that moment. Perhaps my appreciation grew from memories of recent years when even a trip to the convenience store proved beyond my means. After years of being successful and seemingly financially stable, I had hit rock bottom. I struggled to hold on to what I'd worked so hard for. Fortunately, in time, I was able to once again plant my feet on solid ground and become a multi-million dollar earner as a Business Consultant and Success Coach.

As I inhaled the freedom of financial and emotional independence from the high peak of Mount Wuyi, I began to reflect on how determination, hard work and strategic planning had helped to catapult me from a very dark, low place to another mountaintop. Underlining all of this has been the strong foundation laid for me at an early age by my parents. My parents taught me to accept nothing less than the best and to never settle for a mediocre existence. I have heeded these lessons. In a moment of intense delight, I laughed aloud at the image of myself, a man from a small southern town in America, standing atop a mountain in faraway China.

I was born into a working-class family in Greenville, Mississippi, in the heart of the Mississippi Delta flatlands. Greenville was a very close-knit community, rich in culture, folklore and down-home values. My family instilled the importance of hard work and encouraged an entrepreneurial spirit. As a child, I watched my parents work hard to achieve the American dream of independence and financial stability. It seemed as if the harder they worked, the more they gave back. I remember working the family land with my bare hands, cultivating the soil and planting food for us and for the community. After the garden was in bloom and it was time to enjoy the fruits of our labor, my mother would insist that we share most of our crop with our neighbors. She always wanted to make sure that others had enough. Regardless of how much we gave to others, our family never was in need. As a child, I didn't understand my mother's mentality; why would we give away something that we worked so hard for? As an adult, I realize that my family never missed a meal or suffered even in what seemed to be the hardest times. When you give from your heart and your motives are pure, without expecting anything in return, you will be blessed abundantly.

Growing up in Greenville molded my character. It taught me how to be a giver and a server. It was a small world, but its smallness only gave me a keener appreciation for the larger world in which I would access later.

I spent thirteen years in the music industry, starting out as a concert promoter and eventually owning my own record label. I experienced all the highs that a fast-paced lifestyle in the entertainment industry could afford. I enjoyed a lavish lifestyle of clothes, cars, houses and jewelry. You name it, I had it. I enjoyed taking care of family and friends and not having a care in the world. But as they say in the music business, you're either a hit or you're not. It seems that in the blink of an eye the music scene changed and everyone was looking for a quick hit in order "to get paid." No one wanted to put in the hard work and be creative; everyone wanted fame quick, fast, and in a hurry. The hits stopped coming and my life took a downward turn for the worst, or so I thought. I experienced bankruptcy, foreclosure and repossession. I became emotionally and physically ill. I was stressed for breakfast, lunch and dinner. I couldn't comprehend the fact that I was about to hit a brick wall. My career came crashing down right before my eyes. Hitting rock bottom demanded that I draw on the strength, pride and integrity that my mother and father instilled in me as a young man. I picked myself up, dealt with my circumstance, reprogrammed myself, and prepared for the next phase in my life.

While reading *You Have Permission to Succeed*, you will discover that I am an avid reader. I spend much of my spare time reading material that will foster a healthy advancement to the next level. I would be remiss if I did not proclaim my spiritual belief in God as the Creator and Sustainer of all that exists on earth and beyond. My most cherished book is the Bible, which to me is the book of life, the book of knowledge. More intriguing than any novel or self-help book you will ever read, the Bible is filled with answers, solutions and wisdom that apply to everyday life. The

Bible is based on good, sound doctrine that will help you in maintaining an unshakable foundation. Its teachings are what have helped me through my darkest moments.

One of my favorite people in the Bible is Paul. Paul is a shining example of how affliction and circumstance can sometimes emotionally cripple you with thoughts that cause regression and hinder growth. For years Paul had been burdened with what he described as a "thorn" in his side (2 Cor. 12). Paul begged God to remove the thorn so that he might have what he considered a better quality of life. God refused, explaining that this thorn would actually make Paul stronger. God explained to Paul that hardships would elevate and strengthen him. When faced with difficulty, Paul called on God for strength and God granted him the strength to endure. God said to Paul, [1]"My grace is sufficient for you, for my power is made perfect in weakness." In an answer to God's proclamation, Paul said, "[2]I delight in weaknesses, in insults, in hardships, in persecutions, in difficulties. For when I am weak, then I am strong." Paul's strength is not of his own manifestation, but a gift from God who is our strength.

---

[1] **2 Corinthians 12:9**
[2] **2 Corinthians 12:10**

As I look back on the days when the thorns of bankruptcy, debt and hopelessness pierced my side, I thank God for those thorns because they made me stronger. With this book, my mission is to encourage you to delight in the possibilities of the future and to release the thorns of failure, economic hardship and emotional imprisonment. Through my hardships I have developed an abiding appreciation of life and its many blessings that I hope to share with you in these pages.

You may ask yourself, "How can a man who grew up in rural Mississippi and who experienced devastating setbacks in his professional and personal life help me?" Well, just as the words "Your best thoughts have produced your current results in life" changed my life, I realized that my past and current thinking had gotten me to my current position in life. After hearing those words I knew that I had to make some immediate changes. Now, I want to help you change your life by giving you these words, "You Have Permission to Succeed."

For some, the information that I share with you in this book may serve as a refresher or reminder of information you have already touched upon. For others, this information will be fresh and new and greatly enhance your thinking process as you travel on your road to success.

1

Develop Your Why

"When your 'why' is strong enough, 'how' you achieve your desired goal will not matter."

I can remember sitting in my seat as a first grader with an eager hand raised and waiting to answer the question, "What do you want to be when you grow up?" At six years old I was quite sure that I wanted to be a lawyer. As I grew older, my professional vision changed. But from childhood on, one thing remained the same: the desire to succeed.

As I approached my early twenties, I developed my *why*. I clearly thought through the goals I wanted to achieve in life and why I wanted to accomplish those goals. Professionally, I knew that I wanted to secure a future for myself and my daughters. I knew my family depended on me to provide a safe, healthy and nurturing environment. Living a life consumed with stress and uncertainty would promote a toxic and chaotic environment for my wife and children. My desire was to lead a stress-free life that included me and my family going to bed at night without a care in the world. When you develop your *why*—the strong reason underlying the specific goals you have set for yourself—the *how* will fall into place. When your *why* is strong enough, *how* you achieve your desired goal will not matter.

In May, 2009, *Esquire* magazine published an article titled (Cunningham) "The Ten Best Mothers of All Time." One of its featured mothers was Angela Cavallo who made the headlines when she saved her son's life by singlehandedly lifting the car under which her son was pinned. A woman in her late fifties, she rushed into action after the jack collapsed that had been supporting the 1964 Chevy Impala that her son was working on. Anyone acquainted with vehicles made prior to modern day knows that those cars were made of heavy reinforced steel that could presumably plow through a brick wall virtually unscathed. Angela Cavallo's *why*—the life of her son—enabled her to summon the brute strength necessary to lift a car weighing well over a ton. Your own *why* can have that kind of power.

In the beginning, many of us are like starry-eyed children dreaming of limitless possibilities. The world seems much larger than it really is and the sky infinite. As we grow, we realize that "life" happens, things get in the way and the world begins to seem smaller by the minute.

Typically, once you reach the age of accountability (usually age 18), you are no longer directly influenced by your parents or the ones that raised you. You have achieved a measure of independence from your caregiver's way of thinking and philosophies and from the environment that shaped and molded you into the adult that you have become. This is usually the time that you are forced to decide what path to take in life. During your formative years, you have been encouraged to go to school, acquire a "good" education, get a "good" job and lead a productive and meaningful life.

When you are young and still trying to find your way, you spend restless nights and hectic days trying to figure out what to do with your life. For many, seeking a higher education doesn't seem to fit into their own personal plan. Although getting a college degree is essential to some, it is not a prerequisite for success. I have often said that college is not for everyone; some people just don't fit into the traditional, more formal path of higher learning.

> "Any intelligent fool can make things bigger, more complex, and more violent. It takes a touch of genius -- and a lot of courage -- to move in the opposite direction."
>
> -Albert Einstein-

Like most parents, mine instilled in me the importance of a good education. Upon graduation from high school, I did just what I thought I was supposed to do: I enrolled in college. Each day I would attend class and study hard, just as I thought I should. But with every passing day, I became more and more consumed with a feeling of something lacking. I was, indeed, having the classic college classroom experience; I was calculating figures and learning historical facts that saturated the pages of my costly textbooks. After my first year of college, I realized that I wanted to be my own boss and that a formal education was hindering my progress.

My intention is not to discourage anyone from making higher education a goal. If you are able and willing and wanting to attend an institution of higher learning, I wholeheartedly encourage you to seek and accomplish that goal. I simply want to open a doorway in your mind to allow for other possibilities. In my case, I chose an alternate route and my education has been broad and deep. It's taken me, and continues to take me, where I want to go.

So often, people attend a college or university with high expectations that don't mesh with reality upon or after graduation. Students make it through the hectic life of being a college freshman and go on to receive their academic degrees only to realize later that they are still struggling to make ends meet or to climb a corporate ladder that seems unreachable. Those who choose not to attend college may go on to receive an excellent education from the "school of life." They may be fortunate enough to develop common sense, a highly undervalued quality and one often taken for granted. Common sense is the least used sense of all. In having it, I have found, whether you've gone to college or not, anything is possible.

A person may possess an abundance of textbook knowledge but have no idea how to successfully apply it in business or everyday life. Uncombined with common sense and the wisdom of life experience, an individual's hard-won classroom knowledge may remain vacuum-packed and inaccessible. The regrettable outcome can be a highly educated, unsuccessful person.

For quite some time the U.S. has been experiencing an economic downturn that has affected most Americans. Companies continue to outsource and, as technology becomes more

5

advanced, people are replaced by machines and automated recordings. With the rising cost of education, many are forced to figure out an alternative path to survival and success. These realities and stress factors raise the vital question, "Is college really necessary?"

For some the answer is "no". Although obtaining a higher education when coupled with positive life experience and business acumen can only enhance your quality of life, making the choice not to go to college is perfectly acceptable. You are well within your right to choose this option. If you're still a little skeptical and you're feeling pressured to make a choice that you know is not right for you, perhaps some inspiration will do you well.

Thriving in America and across the Atlantic today are a number of high-profile, highly successful individuals who either dropped out of college before finishing or chose not to attend at all. Among these remarkable leaders are Mary Kay Ash, the founder of Mary Kay, Inc.; Richard Branson, the founder of the Virgin brand, which includes Virgin Airlines; Michael Dell, the founder of Dell, Inc.; Bill Gates, the founder of Microsoft, philanthropist, and one of the world's wealthiest people; Walt Disney; and Henry Ford.

At eighteen years old, the phenomenal athlete Lebron James made the decision to forgo his college education to enter the National Basketball Association. James was criticized for his decision. Critics argued that he lacked the experience and maturity that college would provide. To date, James continues to make record-breaking strides in the arena of professional sports. With great determination, undeniable talent, impeccable skill and common sense, he has broken through the stigmatic limitations on success to prove the nay-sayers wrong.

There are also influential people who've done the reverse, putting higher education first of only to pursue a more nontraditional career in later years. Before becoming an actor, philanthropist, and author, Hill Harper had obtained an undergraduate degree from Brown University followed by a *Juris Doctor* degree from Harvard Law School. He is a great example of successfully coupling formal education with life experience in order to take a "road less travelled." Typically, people are afraid of the unknown and of traveling outside the box. From infancy we are encouraged to enter traditional, supposedly safe, professions. Drilled into our heads is the imperative that we must become a doctor, lawyer, nurse, accountant or something considered secure. At this point, the rapid decline in today's economy proves that nothing is secure.

Whatever path you choose, seek sound and wise counsel from someone who has manifested the results, the kind of life and work that you desire. If your path in life does not include a college education or an advanced degree, it is very important that you find a competent, knowledgeable and successful mentor. Finding the right mentor will help you remain focused while you navigate your road to success. Most important, use your common sense, follow through on your *why,* and never let anyone or anything suppress your dream.

LIST YOUR SUCCESS MOTIVATORS

1._____

_____

2._____

_____

3._____

_____

4._____

_____

5._____

_____

6._____

_____

7._____

_____

2

VISUALIZE YOUR SUCCESS

"Part of visualizing your success is to live it every day and dream of it every night."

If you have carefully evaluated your *why* and you've identified your strengths and aspirations regarding your educational path, your next step is to visualize your success and to seek it wholeheartedly. For most people this step is the most difficult. You may ask yourself, "How am I going to get what I want?" Initially, you may lack the experience or resources to get what you desire. These factors should not be used as an excuse to just let your dreams die. You should always be able to see success in your future. You should always know exactly where you want to be at any given time in your life. It's like taking a trip; you should always know your precise destination.

It should seem natural to go through life knowing exactly where you want to end up. The picture for your life and its outcome should be clearly written on paper and spoken into

11

existence. There should be such a strong conviction that if someone were to read your written goals, he or she would be able to sense the emotions and intensity as strongly as you do. The plan for your life should play out like a carefully crafted major motion picture made for the big screen as the events of your life unfold into a well-defined masterpiece. You should make a solid commitment to your plan for achieving success and see it through beyond fruition.

The key to visualizing your success is living it every day and dreaming of it every night. You should see your future as clearly as you see your hand in front of your face. One of the greatest athletes and businessmen in history, Michael Jordan, said that he could see his shots going in to the basket before they were made. The common factor between Jordan and the aforementioned models of success is that they lived and believed that they could do absolutely anything. They owned and claimed their success.

Sometimes I reflect on hearing the term "prayer closet" while attending church and Bible study. This may sound a tad bit odd, but I take the phrase literally. On occasion, when my mind is bogged down with mottled thoughts and I am facing a critical decision, I go into my actual closet and think things through. For me, my closet serves as a refuge. It is quiet and free from outside influences. I take the time to sit and clearly think through the issue and picture just what I want and need. Oddly enough, the closet helps me to erase all the mindless debris, thus fostering a clear path toward resolution. I highly recommend finding your own source of solitude or refuge, where you can clear your mind and focus calmly on what matters most, where you can visualize your success.

Once you have visualized your success, you must then visualize the road ahead and take a clear account of what you need to do to realize your dream. You should be mindful that anything worth having takes hard work and dedication. Also keep in mind that things don't always come easy and there may be obstacles that impede your progress. You should clearly visualize how you will overcome obstacles and remain on the path to success.

When you visualize your success, you should always visualize your desired reward for hard work, determination and unyielding faith. Your desired success and the end result should become a permanent part of you. Burn your success goals into your brain matter until they become a living and breathing portion of your existence. Your success goals need to remain conscious in order to push you forward to the next level. This is called "being in the zone." Once you are in the zone, your vision becomes your reality.

3

SET SPECIFIC GOALS

"Don't watch your dream fade like a dimming light; own your success and take massive action."

N ow that you have developed a *why* and visualized your success, your next step is to set specific goals. Setting goals is perhaps the most important step in achieving success. You must remember that it's not enough to just dream about success. You must put your plan into action. One of the key causes of a deferred dream is poor planning, lack of commitment and lackluster enthusiasm toward achieving your desired goal. Don't watch your dream fade like a dimming light; own your success and take massive action. Habakkuk 2:2 says, "Then the Lord replied: Write down the revelation and make it plain on tablets so that a herald may run with it. For the revelations awaits an appointed time; it speaks of the end and will not prove false.

Though it linger, wait for it; it will certainly come and will not delay."

The first step in setting goals is to write down at least ten goals that you would like to accomplish. In addition to writing down the goals on paper, write down a specific time in which you would like to accomplish each goal. You should view writing your goals as a major accomplishment. Most people think that writing your goals down is trivial, but in fact, this gives you a clear map toward your success. Writing them succinctly suggests that you have a clear understanding of what you want and a reference point for accomplishing your desired success. When setting your goals, remember your *why* and continue to picture exactly what you want.

"Leaders aren't born, they are made. And they are made just like anything else, through hard work. And that's the price we'll have to pay to achieve that goal, or any goal."

-Vince Lombardi-

The journey toward success is paved with a long winding road of various twist and turns. You should approach goal-setting as if you are taking a road trip. Goals serve as a symbolic road map toward reaching your final destination of success. Goals are your mile markers; they will plot your course. Clearly writing out your goals gives you a point of reference and serves as visual motivation. When taking any trip, the anticipation of reaching your destination and the unexpected obstacles that inevitably occur along the way can make the journey challenging. In other words, to use an old cliché, the road to success is paved with potholes. Do not allow them to discourage you. Overcoming obstacles will make you stronger. If you encounter no potholes on the path, you're probably not going anywhere.

Be able to review your written goals at any time. Keep them close to you. Keep a copy in your purse, pocket or wallet. If in any moment you find yourself discouraged, pull out the copy of your goals to remind yourself to stay the course and go the distance.

When writing down your goals, categorize them into two sections: short-term and long-term goals. Make some easily attainable short-term goals and more comprehensive long-term life goals. Be sure to write down your desired time frame for completing each goal. For example, "I will purchase a new house by the end of this year." (Set a specific date.) As you make your list, write your goals in the first-person. "*I* will complete writing my list of goals by..." Using the first-person voice keeps your goals personal, shifts the goal from the abstract to the concrete, and imparts a sense of ownership, which will help you as you progress towards your goal.

In addition to putting your goals down on paper, it is equally important to verbalize them. You might say, for example, "I will earn $100,000 by December 31, ----." Say each goal out loud, with passion and power. Recite your goals as if your life depended on it.

Short-term goals can encompass many small, easily attainable tasks or actions to be completed within a six to twelve-month time frame. Short- term goals might include:

> ❖ **Starting a savings account**
> ❖ **Enrolling in college or going back to college**
> ❖ **Taking a vacation**
> ❖ **Spending more time with your family**
> ❖ **Exercising and eating healthy**

Long-term goals are accomplished over a more extensive period of time. Long-term goals may take *at least* twelve months to achieve. It is common practice when embarking on a new business venture, for example, to prepare a two-year forecast. Of course, this particular goal might be accomplished prior to the two-year mark, but two years allow ample time to properly prepare. Long-term goals might include:

- ❖ **Obtaining a college degree**
- ❖ **Saving $200,000**
- ❖ **Starting a family**
- ❖ **Becoming a partner at your firm**
- ❖ **Starting your own business**
- ❖ **Becoming debt free**

As you accomplish each goal, check them off your list. Seeing a clearly-written goal with a line crossed through it or a check mark next to the entry will give you an amazing sense of accomplishment. Think of your goals as years added to your life. With the achievement of each goal you add another year to your existence. Accomplishing your goals will revive you and give you that extra motivation to reach your destination.

For extra flair, mark your completed goals with a red pen or marker. I know you remember how it felt in grade school to see a big "A" written on your paper in red. Red is a bold symbol of completion. Completing your goals should be one of the most rewarding experiences, giving you a tremendous and empowering sense of accomplishment. Think of how liberating it will be when you have completed your journey and have successfully navigated your road to success.

4

STAY THE COURSE

"Most people become jaded by the amount of effort required to reach the top. It is important that you stay the course. If you run out of gas, fill up. If you hit a brick wall, knock it down."

We live in a fast-paced society filled with instantaneous methods of handling everyday tasks. We rush through everything. We drive in the fast lane racing to get to our destination. We impatiently blow our horns at people who aren't moving fast enough through the green light. We eat instant meals cooked in a microwave, drink instant coffee, and want instant results to complex problems. The ideal situation would be to just have what you desire at your fingertips immediately. Some feel that it is better to win fast like the hare rather than win slow like the tortoise. Although winning fast is good for instant gratification, your pace is not what's most important; the most important thing is that you ran the race. Anyone that goes through the process and finishes at any pace is a winner.

Success takes dedication, proper planning, hard work and perseverance. Most people become jaded by the amount of effort required to reach the top. It is important that you stay the course. If you run out of gas, fill up. If you hit a brick wall, knock it down.

"Life is all about timing... the unreachable becomes reachable, the unavailable become available, the unattainable... attainable. Have the patience, wait it out. It's all about timing."

-Stacey Charter-

When you feel yourself running on empty, remember your *why*. Remember your purpose, review your goals, and get back on that road that leads to a brighter future. Imagine driving on your trip. As you reach each milestone, getting closer to your destination, you become excited. It is very unlikely that you will turn around and go back to your starting point if you are closer to your desired destination and the journey's end. Nothing in life is guaranteed and with each journey there will be the possibility of obstacles deterring your progress. One of the most common obstacles is oneself. It seems that for most, the closer you get to your destination the harder it becomes to see the end of the road. Pay attention to the passing milestones and not the potholes. Be willingly to stay the course, trust that the finish line is near and waiting.

You are on your own time. If others seem to pass, just stay in your lane: Remember that this is your life, these are your goals, and you are the star in your own major motion picture. If you see others driving along in the fast lane, passing you by as if their life is worry-free, as if they have everything in the world, you may begin to wonder, "Why not me?" Just stay the course. You must remember not to take things at face value; everything may not always be what it seems. Remember the time-tested adage, "Everything that glitters is not gold."

One helpful way to bring you closer to your goal is to take the opportunity to stop and ask others how they reached theirs. Don't be afraid to seek advice from others that have advanced to the level you desire. Remember that your fate is ahead of you and only you can hinder yourself from obtaining the success that you desire. If others seem to pass you by, stay the course and remain on the right road, *your* road.

True commitment is staying with something far beyond the disappearance of initial enthusiasm. As you continue to travel on your journey toward the finish line and you discover that you may be losing momentum, pull out a picture of your family, your dream house, or your bank statement, and remember your *why.* Stay committed and be persistent. This is the signal to shift gears and put the pedal to the metal and go full speed ahead. Take some time to regroup and get back on task. A good source of motivation is remembering back to the seemingly desolate rut that you were in before you began your journey. The discomfort of that earlier rut will likely be greater than the current pain of pushing forward. Always remember that at this point you may not be where you want to be, but you're sure not where you once were!

Winning fast vs. Winning slow: We all know the story of the tortoise and the hare. The hare was confident in winning the race because he was fast by nature. The hare was so confident that he would outrun the tortoise, in fact, that he decided to take a nap, thereby taking his eye off the goal. The tortoise, on the other hand, although slow by nature, kept his eye on the prize, remained steady, persevered, and persistent and won the race. As long as you stay committed, stay the course, and continue to envision the finish line, you will still reach your desired destination.

> "If you're trying to achieve, there will be roadblocks. I've had them; everybody has had them. But obstacles don't have to stop you. If you run into a wall, don't turn around and give up. Figure out how to climb it, go through it, or work around it."
>
> -Michael Jordan-

Yes, it is true that staying the course can be difficult. However, if you are willing to commit twenty to thirty years working to build someone else's company, it should seem only logical that you invest that same time and energy on your own dream. Why spend your life working to help someone else gain 95% while you gain only 5%? Although the numbers add up, the

25

scale is obviously one-sided. If you stop and think about it, you may have spent all or most of your adult lifetime supporting someone else's dream, padding someone else's bank account, paying someone else's mortgage, and increasing someone else's net worth. Now it's time to ask yourself, "What sense does that really make?" The answer is plain: it makes no sense at all! The sensible and most logical methodology would be to stay the course and invest two to three years in the most important commodity in the world: "YOU!"

5

BE PREPARED FOR A CHANGE

"Let go of dead weight, assign 'limited access' to those needed, and cleanse yourself of toxic, unproductive relationships."

This is perhaps one of the most important chapters. Most people who actively want to be successful actually dream of success. They live it, breathe it, and see their destination like the clarity of cut crystal. Success does not happen by chance; it is destined. The question that you must ask is, "Am I ready for my destiny?"

As mentioned in the previous chapter, it's easy to wonder why everyone else appears to be moving closer to their destiny while you feel you are coasting along, drifting, in the slow lane. The answer is simple: you have to be prepared to make a change. And making a change is never easy. It has everything to do with trusting yourself and the ability to accept change. God wants us, as his children, to bear fruit (Romans 7:4). God wants us to be abundantly blessed, but He has to know that He can trust us with what He has in store for us.

For years I worked hard toward finding my niche, finding what would make me successful in life. For most of my work life I've been an entrepreneur. I've invested a great deal of time, energy and money in various business ventures. I've gone from one extreme to the next, from owning fine cars, homes, jewelry, and expensive clothes all the way to going through foreclosure, bankruptcy and repossession. One day during the bleaker extreme, I looked around and asked myself, "How did I get here?" How did all my hard work get me to a state of despair and uncertainty? After taking a long serious look at myself and my life at that moment, I realized that I needed to change. I needed to change what I read, what I listened to, and the people I associated with.

Shopping is a way of life, whether you shop on the internet, at a designer boutique, the flea market or the mall. Everyone, regardless of social standing, loves a great bargain. Recently, I was driving around searching for the perfect reading chair for my study. As I arrived at what I hoped would be my last furniture store, I saw a sign in the window that read "Sale." I pulled my car into the parking lot and entered the store. Sale signs were posted everywhere. I browsed throughout, but as in all the other stores, I didn't find what I was searching for. I was just about to leave when I spotted a small backroom full of odds and ends and there sat the perfect chair—the right size, the right color. A sign on the chair read "As Is." A salesperson approached and explained somewhat apologetically that the chair was a final sale item because of an imperfection. I examined the chair carefully and saw what could be and not what was. I concluded that the chair could be repaired and made good as new for minimal cost. It was a superb deal.

The salesperson stood by awkwardly, no doubt ready to be rid of this flawed bit of inventory that was just taking up space. I turned and told him I wanted the chair. To make certain I understood the terms, he repeated that the sale would be final and the chair was being sold "As Is." I paid, loaded the chair into my truck and headed home. On the way I stopped to purchase the materials I would need to touch up the imperfections.

I have since enjoyed numerous hours of reading in that "As Is" chair. Just think, if I had passed it by because of its shortcomings, I would have missed out on a blessing.

I encourage you to ask yourself whether you want to leave yourself behind in a dusty backroom wearing an "As Is" sign that attests to your mistakes, failures and fears. Anyone can improve himself or herself and work toward becoming more attractive, inside and out. You can refuse to allow real or perceived imperfections to define you or to dictate your future worth.

Being attractive encompasses much more than your physical appearance. It includes attributes such as becoming more knowledgeable in your career/business, adapting a more positive attitude concerning life, improving people skills, belief in oneself, mastering the art of communication, developing a larger vision and maintaining unyielding focus. The laws of attraction influence your ability to draw the right people and opportunities to you.

As human beings that have been granted free will, we have the choice to stay as we are or to improve ourselves. There is always room for improvement in our professional, personal and spiritual lives. When I was a child, my mother always told me, "God don't make no junk." If God has created you as special and worthy, if that is your innate God-given nature, as it is mine, then we must do no less than to cultivate that nature.

The chair I bought and refurbished had much greater value than it was credited for. It had been hidden away and labeled as lacking. Yet somehow, to me, it stood out as special and I was able to see beneath the surface and recognize its inherent value and its potential to be the perfect chair.

> "Surround yourself with only people who are going to lift you higher."
>
> -Oprah Winfrey-

Sometimes people can see something in us that we cannot see in ourselves. When we encounter someone who makes a conscious effort to support us, who encourages us, we should hold on to that gift and allow that person's positive influence into our lives. When navigating your path to success, it is exceeding helpful to have someone by your side in the passenger seat reviewing your map with you and watching you pass each milestone.

Once I decided that I needed to prepare myself for change, I sat down and began to analyze various aspects of my life. I started by taking a look at the people I was spending most of my time with. I sat down and compiled a list of my friends and associates and wrote down both the positive and negative aspects of each relationship. This process was quite difficult yet eye-opening. I'd known some of these people for a long time. But once I thought long and hard about myself and the path that I chose to take, I cleared my mind and heart. I realized that most of my relationships were toxic (negative) and only hindered me from reaching my full potential. Many of these people could not travel with me on my road to success.

Often, as a source of security, we hold on to people simply because it feels comfortable and familiar. Sometimes people enter our lives only for a season or a particular reason. Once that season or reason has ended, it is okay to cherish the memories and let go with grace and respect.

I am in no way encouraging anyone to abandon friends and family if they don't share your vision or ideas. Family and friends can be bedrock foundational elements in your life. You may not share the same goals, but family and friends can still remain constant and always support you.

But there will be those in your life to whom you want to give only "limited access." This means consciously setting boundaries. In other words, certain people will only be as close to you as you allow them to be. Evaluate your relationships. Let go of dead weight, assign "limited access" as needed, and cleanse yourself of unproductive relationships.

I encourage you to enhance your life by seeking like-minded individuals who share and understand your vision. Surround yourself with positive people who offer constructive criticism, heartfelt encouragement and sound advice. Remember, successfully connecting with people who share your passion and determination depends upon your willingness to let go of negative and unproductive relationships. Stick with the winners.

If the task of reevaluating and eliminating some people in your life seems overwhelming, think of it as a pruning process. When I was a boy, my mother grew many different types of house plants. On weekends she and I would move the plants from the sunroom to the backyard where we watered them and removed their dead leaves. If necessary, we also replanted any flowers that had outgrown their original pots. Then, when finished, we would have to hang all the plants back up in the sunroom. Each weekend, this was my assigned chore as a child.

In the beginning, it seemed a tedious and meaningless task to me. I would complain about having to take the heavy plants in and out of the sunroom. Finally one day, I asked my mother why we were cutting off the brown portions of the leaves. My mother explained to me that cutting the dead portions of the leaves allows a plant to flourish. The process was called pruning, she said.

> **Books and Music**
>
> 1. Create a personal library.
>
> 2. Reading inspires change, motivates positive thinking and encourages knowledge, personal power, Communication skills and cognition.
>
> 3. Select the books that you read and the music you listen to very carefully.
>
> 4. What you listen to can affect your thoughts and actions.
>
> 5. Reading is fun!

Pruning removes dead, diseased and other unhealthy bits from a plant so that it can thrive and grow. Just as with plants, we cannot live healthy and productive lives without pruning whatever dead leaves have accumulated. Think of yourself as the healthy green leaves of a plant that crave water, food and sunlight. Now recognize that some of the individuals in your life may be standing in the way, intentionally or unintentionally, of you obtaining what you need to flourish.

After honestly evaluating my current relationships, I made a list of people I admire. I wrote down the particular characteristics that I esteemed in each of these individuals and consciously began to adopt those traits into my behavior and life. Does this make me a copycat? I hope so. My motto is that it's alright to be a copycat as long as you copy the right cat! Perhaps one of the most amusing facts about my journey is when I began to associate with positive-minded, forward-moving individuals, I became one of them.

Another aspect of preparing for change that I cannot stress enough is the importance of reading—and paying particular attention to *what* you read. The brain is like an absorbent sponge. When we read, we take in every word, thought and image. It is reasonable to assume that whatever we read becomes a part of us. When we read negative literature, empty of any real meaning, it has an impact. We absorb the negative content and, eventually, the surplus of negative thoughts become a negative reality.

Until a few years ago, I wasn't interested in reading any-thing. I wouldn't even read the sports section of the newspaper. But once I began the quest for a better quality of life my thirst for knowledge increased and I began to read—especially positive, motivational and spiritual material. I even read a book on how to improve my reading. The reading habit, now that I've found it, is one I suspect will never leave me now.

As a catalyst and support for change, I believe that listen-ing to positive personal development audio recordings to be equally as powerful as reading. People who have difficulty reading are often able to easily comprehend and absorb information through listening. The music we listen to has a greater influence on us than we realize, and just as we must be discerning in what we read, we also need to choose our music mindfully. One of the major debates that continue to surface in our society is the negative influence that some music has on our children. Some criminals have even blamed certain songs for the crimes they've committed. This has become a growing epidemic.

Music is designed to encourage or enhance a certain mood. Love songs are designed to promote a romantic encounter with your significant other. Upbeat songs encourage us to dance and have a good time. As we head to the dance floor, we allow the rhythm, beat and lyrics to enter our minds and bodies and transport us to euphoria. But as in any medium, music can have a negative as well as a positive aspect. Music filled with negative lyrics encourages negative thinking.

At times, I find myself bobbing my head mindlessly to senseless songs on the radio, professing to liking the beat. Fortunately, my good sense kicks in and I quickly change the station or pop in one of my personal development CD's. Truthfully, once you begin to passionately seek change, you will do whatever is needed to make things happen.

I have listened to thousands of hours of personal development and motivational CD's. This has allowed me to saturate my mind with positive ideas and experiences to help to dissolve the negative influences that have clouded my mind for many years.

As a final element of making a change, let's talk about appearance. I'm sure you're thinking that appearance has everything to do with the way you dress. Unfortunately, in today's society people continue to judge others based on appearance. First impressions continue to be the basis of building future business and personal relationships. It's the law of attraction—the ability to draw people and opportunities closer to you. My mother has always told me that being neat and clean is priceless. She taught me to walk upright, not to slouch, hold my head up, and deliver a firm handshake.

I'd like to relate a lighthearted story from one of my favorite television shows when I was growing up—"The Cosby Show." The Huxtable's appeared to have it all together, the image of everything a good old American family should be. I was partial to the character Vanessa, one of the daughters, who was articulate and intelligent and always telling her brothers and sisters how they should act. In one episode, Vanessa returns home from her first year of college with an unexpected guest. She was accompanied by a fiancé ten years her senior. No one in the family knew that Vanessa was engaged and the existence of her fiancé was a total shock. Parents Cliff and Claire were livid and riddled with reservations. The entire family sits down to dinner, including the fiancé, and Cliff explains to Vanessa that it isn't the choice she's made, but the way she presented it.

Cliff offers the analogy of how much he enjoys a good steak. He describes his ideal steak as a piping hot porterhouse, rich with herbs and spices, covered in mushrooms and onions, and cooked to tender perfection to please any palate. Everyone's mouth waters as they listen, rapt, until Cliff delivers the *coup de grace* to make his point. The fantasy steak, so lovingly conjured up, is served not upon a magnificent plate but rather upon the lid of an unwashed garbage can. Cliff's point was that, the analogy wasn't about Vanessa bringing her fiancé to dinner; it was about how he was presented to the family. Remember, that it is all about proper presentation. If your idea or plan is properly presented, it is a greater possibility that it will be accepted leading you one step closer to success.

In referring to presentation, I am in no way insisting or encouraging you to go out and purchase a $1,500 suit and a pair of $500 shoes. If you only have one shirt, one pair of pants, one skirt or dress, or one pair of shoes, just make sure that your ensemble is neat, clean and fresh each time you wear it. Dressing for success is an important part of your journey.

Appearance is more than what you wear. It includes your social skills as well. Make sure you are respectful in conversation, listen, make eye contact and don't interrupt the person talking. Be sure not to be overbearing or offensive. Stay away from jokes that touch upon religion, race or sexuality. Relating skillfully is especially important if you are establishing a rapport with someone you've never met before and may know nothing about. You can't always anticipate when someone might be offended by your words.

As I stated earlier, first impressions are the basis of forming lasting relationships. Handshakes are very important. Make sure you greet people with a firm handshake; there is nothing worse than the "wet fish handshake." The wet fish handshake is cold and clammy and screams "gross!" The wet fish handshake can also reveal that you are extremely nervous and unsure of yourself. On the other hand, please don't use your hand as a vise grip, crippling or cutting off the circulation of the other's hand. Make sure that your handshake is quick and comfortable. Confidently extend your hand. Hold the other person's hand firmly, count to three and then release it.

Your extended, shaking hand should be on top. Tilt the receiver's hand just a little. Make it easy and relaxed. Shaking hands should not be a struggle or battle. If by chance you cannot position your hand on top, just remain confident and conscious of your actions. You may ask, "Why all this concern about a hand-shake?" Sometimes a simple handshake can make the difference between a quick hello-and-goodbye and a long lasting relationship.

With all that I've talked about in this chapter, the most important thing for you to remember is that in order for things in your life to change, *you* must change.

Appearance:

1. Keep your clothes ironed and pressed. Wrinkled clothing shows that you don't think much of yourself or the opportunity being presented.

2. Men and women should maintain neat well-groomed hair. Keep it simple. For men facial hair should always be kept neat.

3. Hands should be clean. Keep your nails trimmed. Don't wear nails too long; keep them at an "active length." Don't bite your nails; doing so shows signs of extreme nervousness and insecurity.

4. Perfume or cologne can be offensive. If worn, make sure your fragrance does not enter the room before you do.

5. Remember where you're going. If it's business, don't dress like you're going to a party, the club, a wedding, or even a funeral. Maintain professional attire at all times. Don't overdo it.

6. Surprisingly, shoes are one of the first things people notice. Make sure that your shoes are clean and polished. Do not wear shoes with scuff marks or worn heels and toes.

7. Men should wear a brown or black belt that is free from tears or frayed edges.

8. Women should carry a simple and classic handbag that says you're focused more on business than the latest fashion trend. Remember to keep it simple and classy!

9. Most important appearance has everything to do with attitude. Be confident in who you are and everything else will fall into place.

IDENTIFY THE THINGS THAT YOU NEED TO CHANGE
(Include your name and why you need to change)

I _____ will change:

_____

_____

_____

_____

I _____ will change:

_____

_____

_____

_____

I _____ will change:

_____

_____

_____

_____

I _____ will change:

_____

_____

_____

_____

I _____ will change:

_____

_____

_____

_____

I _____ will change:

_____

_____

_____

_____

6

MASTER YOUR FEARS

"Mental imprisonment can be more detrimental than physical imprisonment. Step outside of your emotional jail cell and set your sights on personal and financial freedom."

On March 4, 1933, the nation's thirty-second president, Franklin Delano Roosevelt, stood before a crowd of thousands to give his inaugural address. With a confident spirit and the powerful presence of hope, Roosevelt stood before a nation of people stifled by a depression to render a speech that would become one of the most poignant speeches in history.

As he stood behind the podium staring out into the faces of an American public that trusted him to deliver them from a crippling economy and an uncertain future, Roosevelt held his head high and said, "...[F]irst of all, let me assert my firm belief that the only thing we have to fear is fear itself..."

> "The only thing we have to fear is fear itself…"
>
> -Franklin Delano Roosevelt-

In the nearly eighty years since its delivery, this single line has become a source of motivation and strength for countless numbers of people setting out to face their fears. One of the most common hindrances to success is fear. Fear is an ironic emotion that drives some and cripples others. There are those who fear failure and others who are simply afraid of the unknown. Fear can be a driving force that motivates one to work harder than the average person to achieve a goal. Those afraid of failing are often driven to succeed. Those afraid of the unknown or afraid of stepping outside of their comfort zone often freeze up and never reach their full potential. Fear of the unknown can lead to the "what if" syndrome— endless thoughts of wondering what could have happened if we hadn't been afraid to take a chance and step out into the unknown with faith, God-given talent, and determination. The most important factor in conquering fears is to determine whether the fear is a fear of success or a fear of failure.

FEAR OF SUCCESS

Fear of being successful can be considered as an unconscious sabotage of your own progress. When you fear success, you unconsciously make excuses for why you have not reached your desired goal. Fear of success can include constant procrastination to execute things that can help catapult you to the next level. For example, most of us feel motivated to make a change at the beginning of a new year. If January turns to May without your having taken the necessary steps toward starting a new business, for example, then you qualify as a procrastinator. Procrastinators make excuses for why they have not moved forward, have not yet secured that business name or applied for an EIN(Employee Identification Number) number or even finished the business plan. Procrastination and excuses go hand-in-glove and are proficient at eroding one's dreams, at undermining the fulfillment of one's goals.

Goals are like flowers. People plant flowers to enhance their property, to add value to the home into which they've invested much time, energy, and money. Each planting season countless hours are spent perusing nurseries and home improvement stores for just the right flower or shrub. People pride themselves on the display of colors and beauty of the flowers in their gardens. Nurturing every bloom are the dedication and patience, the vision and meticulous labor of the gardener. Your personal goals require no less. Think of any fears that arise as equivalent to weeds in a garden. They can either overrun the garden or they can be tamed. Know that you have a choice. You can either cultivate your dreams or you can cultivate your fears. You can't do both.

The fear of success manifests itself in various ways. Sometimes it's a fear of attracting too much attention or fanfare. Some people are private and reserved by nature. They choose to lead simple lives hidden from the public eye. They choose to fly under the radar. The fear of gaining too much attention hinders their success.

Others fear that they cannot trust themselves with increased financial responsibilities. In order to assist with your fear of gaining more financial responsibility, you should seek the advice of a sound financial advisor that will help you stay on track. Some people fear that the chaos they feel now will follow them into success. People worry about their ability to maintain a hectic schedule and withstand the pressures and hustle and bustle that come with added responsibility. The increased expectations on oneself can be daunting. In order to maintain a hectic schedule practice prioritizing your tasks. Don't take on to many tasks at once, simply take one step at a time.

I encourage you to stop standing at the window of your glass house watching others enjoy the fruits of their labor. Step out, breath in the fresh air, and enjoy life. Gaining more attention does not need to be a negative. Use the attention to your advantage; take this as a networking opportunity to meet new people and place yourself in positive situations.

FEAR OF FAILURE

The fear of failure or, as it is clinically called; Atychiphobia is a common phenomenon. It can be quite deceitful and lead down two different roads—one constructive, the other destructive. When its impact is positive, the fear of failure can stimulate a person to succeed and to exceed his or her limitations. In those cases, the fear of failure serves as a powerful motivator toward action. People so driven will almost always succeed.

In its negative aspect, the fear of failure can keep a person stuck and passively waiting on the sidelines for a windfall to appear. It may paralyze a person even in the initial step of setting goals. Unvaryingly, beneath the fear of failure lies a deep belief in the impossibility of one's own success. This combination can stall a person indefinitely, or even permanently. When under the spell of fears and self-defeating beliefs, people can easily conclude— consciously or subconsciously—that their goals, visions and dreams were just a passing fantasy, a kind of mirage. It's a misconception that unattended dreams die or fade away. On the contrary, once you have given birth to your vision, it becomes a part of you and lives with you every single moment. The constant nagging in your head, the perpetual whisper to work toward your goal, is your dream fighting to come alive. Dreams don't die, they're just deferred.

The late African American poet Langston Hughes dedicated an entire series of poems to dreams, one of his most notable poems is titled (Hughes)"A Dream Deferred". This poem takes an analytical view of what takes place when a dream is put on hold. In his poem, Hughes does not allude to what may have caused the dream to be deferred. Dreams can be deferred by a number of things. Never allow distractions to infiltrate and unconsciously maneuver you away from your path. Hughes gives a graphic illustration of a dream that has been put on the back burner. He addresses this issue in a series of questions that poses an unconventional look at the impending death of a dream. You should think of the fear of failure as something that is detrimental to your growth and development as a successful person.

> A Dream Deferred
>
> What happens to a
> dream deferred?
> Does it dry up
> like a raisin in the
> sun?
> Or fester like a sore--
> And then run?
> Does it stink like
> rotten **meat**?
> Or crust and sugar
> over--
> like a syrupy sweet?
> Maybe it just sags
> like a heavy load.
> Or does it explode?
>
> **-Langston Hughes-**

> "Freedom of mind is the real freedom. A person whose mind is not free though he may not be in chains, is a slave, not a free man. One whose mind is not free, though he may not be in prison, is a prisoner and not a free man. One whose mind is not free though alive, is no better than dead. Freedom of mind is the proof of one's existence."
>
> -Unknown-

When it comes to any type of fear, whether it's the fear of success or the fear of failure, we are often our own worst enemy. Fear is a state of mind that can function as a kind of prison that holds our insecurities as well as our strengths. Mental imprisonment can be more detrimental than physical imprisonment. We set limits on ourselves because of past experiences and the uncertainties of the unknown. We tell ourselves that we can't do something or can never attain our desired goals. To convince ourselves that "we can't," we conform to circumstances such as not having enough money, not thinking we are good enough or just a plain old lack of confidence.

During your journey, it is important not only to seek encouragement from your family or friends or a mentor, but also to encourage yourself. You must be in your own corner. Step outside of your emotional jail cell and set your sights on personal and financial freedom.

7

MASTER LEADERSHIP

"True leadership is when others follow you even when they don't have to."

The year 2007 proved to be the beginning of a long journey toward an overdue change, not just in the United States, but in the entire world. In February, 2007, a long and lean African American gentleman with an exotic look and an indelible name emerged as a front-runner in the 2008 presidential election. No African American had ever before risen to the presidency. What was the likelihood that candidate Barack Obama would ascend to this country's highest honor? Statistically and historically, the odds of a young African American male born to a Kenyan father and an Anglo mother winning the highest seat in the land seemed impossible. Yet, Barak Obama emerged as an audacious contender with undeniable leadership ability. His confidence and charisma inspired people not only to believe in him, but also to believe in themselves. Barack Obama's ability to be an effective leader inspired the entire world to welcome a much needed change.

True leadership is when others follow you even when they don't have to. There is a distinct difference between being a leader and being a dictator. Dictators are followed out of fear, but true leaders are followed out of respect. A leader's job is to steer or influence others to work toward obtaining a desired goal. It takes an extraordinary person to convince and inspire others to take action or to follow your lead.

Being a leader means being a leader in every aspect of your life, not just in your professional world. A prerequisite to leadership is the maintenance of your personal, professional and spiritual health. Without that, you cannot expect others to trust you in any aspect of business. A great leader must have a clear vision, purpose and plan for obtaining his or her desired goals. As discussed in Chapter 3, "Visualize Your Success," you must be able to see your vision as clearly as the hand in front of your face. Others will only follow you when you know where you're going, when your footsteps are sure. Many people experience failure in business because they don't wholeheartedly believe in the product they are selling or the business they are building. Leadership is about belief!

As stated in Chapter 1, "Develop Your Why," an effective leader must evaluate the purpose underlying the goals that he or she has set. You must ensure that your purpose is definite and pure. If you base your purpose solely on making money, you risk a greater chance of falling prey to get-rich-quick schemes and traveling from business to business just trying to make a dollar.

As a child, I loved watching my father work to build his business. I was always right by his side trying to learn how to be just like him. It seemed that he did everything with determined effort that consistently produced winning results. I possessed an enduring yearning to be like my father. This yearning could only be nourished by his powerful example. Good leaders do just that: they possess the ability to take people forward, not back.

Leadership generally accompanies the highest paid professions. Typically, the person who serves as the head of the company earns the most money. This is most common in the corporate arena. People at the top of the corporate hierarchy are paid to lead the company and its personnel in a positive and profitable direction. The goal of the business leader is to ensure that the company maintains a high industry ranking, competes effectively, and earns significant profits. These individuals have most likely obtained some form of higher education and have excelled in their field of study. They have gone through extensive training, often moving up through the ranks, and have the proven ability to move the company forward.

At some point leaders will wonder if they are making a positive impact. There are several key indicators of effective leadership. As people demand more of your time and knowledge, your earning potential should increase. There is a significant difference between a "one- dollar" leadership and a "million-dollar" leadership.

The best leaders are those who can relate to a wide variety of personalities. Keeping an open mind and educating yourself on various cultural and regional business practices is very important. I invested in books, videos, DVD's and CD's to aid my learning in how to respect various personalities and communicate skillfully. I had to become a master at identifying with different individuals, an essential quality for an effective leader. Once you develop that necessary skill, your proficiency in the art of persuasion will follow naturally.

Before you can know anyone else, of course, you must first know yourself. You cannot effectively communicate with others if you don't truly know who you are. While reading the book *People Smarts* by Tony Alessandra, I learned not only how to relate to other people, but also how to understand myself. Understanding yourself and how you think is very important.

A key mistake made by aspiring leaders is an inappropriate focus on oneself. The quality of self-centeredness will ultimately derail a person's hopes for leadership. Leadership should never be solely about you—how far you've come, how far you're going. Leadership at its best is about guiding your team in a positive direction. True leaders want to empower their team and to create the conditions that allow team members to develop and prosper. Strong leaders are dedicated to the economic, emotional, and spiritual advancement of their team.

My business partners and I developed an operating philosophy that includes our taking a look at our personal goals once a year. This allows us to finalize our personal goals prior to entering a new year. Most important, this practice allows us to focus on the goals of the team of individuals we serve. Leadership is all about service. We believe that as you advance and acquire a leadership role, you should continue to serve others. True leadership is effectively guiding your team to achieve their desired success. You'll know you're leading effectively if your team has followed your direction and continues to make a significant profit or advance in their career. A positive reflection of your leadership is how well your team performs, collectively and individually.

When you're a leader, remember that people will watch your actions. Whether you want to be or not, people will view you as a role model. Consciously or subconsciously, many will pattern themselves after you. You will always be out-front and center stage. This simply comes with the territory. In addition to your other responsibilities, you are charged with setting a positive example for others, including family and friends. For me, personally and professionally, it's always lights-camera- action.

As a leader, you need exceptional listening skills. In any conversation, always listen first, process the information, and then offer the most thoughtful response. Never give a knee-jerk or spontaneous response to any question. Remember that your response will carry a certain weight and can either help or hurt a situation decisively.

Great leaders are developed. The personal, spiritual, emo- tional, and professional principles you practice will come into play.

Get to know and develop the "leader" inside of you. A great book that helped me to develop the leader inside me was, John C. Maxwell's "Develop The Leader Inside You." Be sure to maintain your personal and professional character. Consciously cultivate your leadership skills. Remember, these are *learned* skills. Becoming a leader is possible for you.

8

MASTER YOUR FINANCES

"Always remember, it's not what you earn; it's what you keep.

Applied wisdom produces wealth."

Mastering your finances is a bottom-line requirement for success. You should always have something to show for all the hard work that you put into building your business or your career. Always remember, it's not what you earn; it's what you keep. After earning millions in the record industry, I had nothing to show for it. After leaving the music industry, it seemed that earning millions was in vain; at some point I could no longer take pleasure in my riches. I had to enjoy it as an afterthought or a memory. People chase after financial freedom daily, but most financial freedom remains elusive.

You should strive to be financially sound not only in the bank, but in principle as well. One of the most important of these principles is to *pay yourself first*. Paying ourselves serves as a reward for our hard work. As a child I remember receiving rewards or treats for things that I had accomplished. Earning a reward was an incentive for me to work even harder.

Sound Financial Principles

1-Reward Yourself for Accomplishing Certain Goals

It is good practice to set up rewards for yourself as you accomplish certain goals. After experiencing financial hardships, one of my goals was to reach a personal monthly income of $40,000. The subsequent reward would be relocating to a particular upscale neighborhood that I found desirable to live in.

2-Tithe 10% - Save 10% - Invest 10%

As a Christian, I firmly believe that God is my business partner. It is written in the Bible that you must give ten percent of your net earnings to God. Therefore, if God is my business partner, it should only seem right that I give Him the ten percent that He requested. If you think about it, you're really getting a great deal it's a 90/10 split. God supplies everything and gives the increase, what a deal! It's the best partnership. Some people review tithing as "just giving" but I hold true to the belief that the more you give, the more you receive. Giving to God willingly demonstrates obedience. The more you trust in God the more He is able to trust you with.

60

In addition to tithing, I recommend putting ten percent of your income into savings. In effect, this means treating your savings like a bill—your biggest bill. Committing to this, for me, was the most difficult financial decision in the beginning. I now view my savings account as my most important creditor. There are some bills that never allow delinquency. You have to have electricity, so you pay your electric bill. If you have to have a car, you pay whatever you must to keep it on the road. To assure your shelter, you pay the rent or mortgage in a timely manner. All of these things are considered necessities for most. Saving at least ten percent of your earnings should be made a necessity and priority as well. No matter how little or how much you earn, practicing this principle is a key step toward financial freedom. If you practice this principle no matter how small the amount, imagine how awesome it will be when your earnings increase.

Investing 10% of your earnings will ensure that your money will make money. Making sound responsible investments is a process that involves extensive research, good counsel and patience. Never make major investment decisions based solely on immediate need or emotions. There are several avenues of investments stocks, bonds, commodities, mutual funds as well as real estate. Whatever avenue you chose, take your time and don't expect unrealistic results. Once you have thoroughly researched investment options, start small with your investments. As your money grows and you gain more experience, gradually increase the types of investments and the amount of money that you invest.

3-It Is More Expensive To Be Broke Than To Be Rich.

When your debt is greater than your income and you are barely making ends meet, you risk falling into a deeper hole that forces you to fight your way out. Notice the difference in lifestyle:

When You Don't Have Money You:

- ❖ You pay late fees
- ❖ Your interest rates are higher
- ❖ You settle for a less desirable area to live in
- ❖ You drive a less desirable and reliable car
- ❖ You live unhealthily because being healthy is often more costly

When You Have Money:

- ❖ You have complimentary services and perks
- ❖ Your interest rates are lower

- ❖ Your choices of a more desirable neighborhood are greater.
- ❖ You drive what you want
- ❖ People are typically much more accommodating (They compete for your business)

4- Have At Least 2-3 Years of Living Expenses Saved.

Ensuring that you save at least two to three years of living expenses serves as an insurance policy in case the unexpected should occur. This safety net would allow you a greater chance of ensuring that your bills continue to be paid and also enable you to rebuild your life, business or career, should that be necessary. This may seem a little overwhelming, but you can start by saving for one month, three months or six months of living expenses. Build your savings in ninety day increments until you reach your desired savings goal.

5-Never Take Advice From Financially Unstable People

Sometimes it amuses me to observe financially unstable people giving financial advice. They seem to know everything, but have no proven results to point to in order to support the wisdom of their advice. If your financial status is less desirable and some-one in the same financial state as you attempts to give you financial advice, that is your number-one clue not to listen! Seek financial advice from someone with a proven track record and of sound financial stature. My motto is, "If your portfolio is not stronger than mine, don't expect me to take your advice."

6-Create a Budget That Works For You

Create a budget for you that works and be sure to stick to it. If you realize that you are not capable of properly managing a set budget, you should seek assistance from a qualified financial adviser.

When it comes to safeguarding and growing your financial resources, remember that it's okay to say no to people and outside influences that may come along and distract you. An item you especially desire may suddenly become available to purchase, for example. But if the item does not fall within the range of your budget, it is okay to say no to yourself and make a positive sacrifice for your future.

Friends and family may come to you and ask for a loan and it is perfectly okay to say no. I am in no way discouraging you from assisting those in need, but sometimes you have to remember that your own needs are just as important. You may need to help others figure out an alternative to borrowing from you. Never put yourself in the position of being unable to help yourself.

Remember that your financial health is as important as your physical health. Troubled finances can add stress and strain that have a negative impact on your physical health. Money can be your friend or your enemy. You must develop the mindset of respecting money. People often stumble into financial ruin because they treated money as if it grew on trees. Make sure that you develop respectful and responsible investment and spending habits.

Learn to build your net worth as well as your self-worth. Most people do their best to build a nest egg and often do so by working for someone else. A nest egg is what you traditionally save in order to live your later years in comfort and security. Yours may be a retirement or 401k plan that is offered by your employer. But, typically, most people don't invest in other options outside of what is available at their place of employment. Building a retirement nest egg is important, but I would like to encourage you to expand your vision to building your net worth. Developing your net worth demands you immediate and full attention.

You have to start somewhere, so there is nothing wrong with working for someone else. Most people are unable to just quit their job and become self-employed. However, while working toward your goal, stay focused and stay the course. While punching a clock or working for an employer, don't lose sight of your own dreams. Participate in activities that will allow you to build the business or portfolio that you desire to own for yourself. Building your net worth means to build an aggressive source of income that will create your desired lifestyle and afford you the opportunity to have what I like to call "disposable income." Put yourself in a position where money is knocking at your door asking for a place to stay.

As you go through life, no matter what avenue you chose to accomplish your desired goal, whether it is the traditional route of seeking a higher education, obtaining a job or being an entrepreneur, build something for yourself. Leave a legacy for your family to be proud of and benefit from. I believe your family should start where you finish, not where you started. Each generation should be more advanced than the other.

Toward building your net worth, I offer these basic guidelines:

❖ Make sure you properly plan for a solid financial freedom
❖ Seek the right investments
❖ Obtain proper health and life insurance
❖ Create some form of residual income (Locate a product or business that is profitable and build it. This will allow you to have steady *walkaway* income).

Start planning now, take financial action, and reap the rewards in your financially free future. Preparing for a financially

67

sound future may seem difficult in the beginning. You may feel some discomfort and feel like you're drowning or barely staying afloat financially. While making sacrifices and preparing for a stable financial future, you may encounter some hardships. It is natural to be concerned about bills, relationships, jobs, and all the other aspects of our human condition. However, time spent worrying is time that can be used to move closer toward your goal. Remember to think and act wisely; don't act on impulse or pure emotion. Remember that applied wisdom produces wealth.

MONTHLY BUDGET

Monthly Income		Monthly Expenses	
Net Income	$	Tithe	$
Gross Income	$	Savings	$
Investments	$	Taxes(business owners)	$
Additional Income	$		
List additional income		List additional monthly expenses	

9

UNDERSTANDING YOUR WORTH

"Just as Michelangelo saw greatness in a piece of stone, there is also a tremendous greatness inside each of us just waiting to emerge."

In an earlier chapter, I advised you to read material of substance, material that is thought-provoking and that challenges you to think outside the box. Recently, I had the pleasure of reading just such a book, *"The Angel Inside,"* by Chris Widener. In Chapter One, "Finding the Angel Inside of You," Tom Cook, a tourist, reaches the final destination of his European tour. Tom has been traveling for quite some time and has reached a point of mental and physical exhaustion. Just as he finds a suitable place to rest his weary soul and feel sorry for himself, he encounters an old man who immediately strikes up a conversation. Feeling annoyed and wishing to be left alone but not wanting to be rude, Tom politely responds to the old man's overtures.

The old man turned Tom's attention to one of the most famous masterpieces known to humankind, Michelangelo's exquisite sculpture of the biblical hero David. Tom was so engaged in self-pity that he did not realize that he was sitting in front of this magnificent work of art. Despite Tom's obvious lack of interest, the old man launched into the story of the creation of the statue. A series of artists had been commissioned to attempt to sculpt David, the old man said, but without success. Their imaginations failed to perceive the possibility of any beauty emerging from the gigantic and rather ordinary looking hunk of rock with which they'd been given to work. One by one, the artists abandoned the project as hopeless. The 26-year-old artist Michelangelo was the next to accept the problematic commission. Unlike the others, he poured his heart and soul into chipping away at this massive stone. He labored with every fiber of his being. When asked why he was working so hard on such a worthless piece of rock, Michelangelo is said to have replied, "There is an angel inside of this rock and I am setting him free."

It took Michelangelo three years to complete the massive, sculpture. From the block of stone, actually a block of marble, emerged the work of art we know today as simply *David*. The old man challenged Tom to see the positive aspects that lie within what most people see as a challenge.

This story touches me deeply because, just as Michelangelo saw something marvelous inside a shapeless piece of stone, something marvelous also exists inside each and every one of us. We are often our own worst enemy, not believing in ourselves enough to step out on faith and dare to thrive and succeed. Each one of us is like that block of raw marble waiting to be chiseled into a masterpiece. Most of us don't clearly understand our own worth. We judge ourselves by our exterior or, looking inside, see only the issues that seem unsolvable. We convince ourselves that the best we can hope to be is mediocre.

Michelangelo knew that what he was working with was much more than it appeared to be. We need to know the same about ourselves. Just being a human being gives us something immeasurably valuable to work with. Everyone is worth something much greater than what can be seen on the outside.

Most people chase success outside themselves and as a kind of dream that culminates in a sea of constant bliss. Much time and energy is spent chasing after the fantasy and looking for something that has been there all along. The pathway and secrets to success—the real thing—lie within.

Success is like a tantalizing dessert that delights the palate. Any good baker knows that sweet treats aren't just made; they are masterfully created with specific ingredients in happy combination. Most cakes require flour, sugar, eggs, flavoring, and butter. Alone, these are just ingredients; together, they make a mouthwatering confection. The basic ingredients for success are faith, determination, hard work and perseverance. Alone, each is useful, but together and combined with the unique human being that is "you", success is inevitable.

As I stated earlier, God is the Creator and Sustainer of everything. It is He who sustains me and has made it possible for me to share my experience with you. I deeply value my self-worth and the fact that just as God created us in his own image, He created us in that same likeness. I believe that we are sons and daughters of the Most High. If we believe in the spirit of being created in God's own image, then why shouldn't we believe in our own self-worth. God valued us enough to put His stamp on us. Shouldn't we value ourselves just as much?

You are the most important person in your business or company; you are your own brand. Everyone is unique and has characteristics that make them extraordinary. There is no one like you in this world and you must encourage yourself to believe that you are a major contributor to this world. One of the most important keys to success is maintaining emotional stability and knowing that you are capable of achieving the goals that you have set for yourself. When fostering a healthy sense of self-esteem, it is important to realize that what others think of you is just that: what they think of you. We often lose ourselves and get caught up in what I call a "they sayers" mentality. We worry about what *they* say about us, how *they* feel about us, and if *they* approve of us.

A sure way of clearing your pathway to success is to free yourself from the negative opinions of others, whether spoken or unspoken. People are always going to form an opinion of you whether it's good or bad, whether you have reached an acceptable level of success or not. If you know your own worth and revel in your greatness, then what they say will not matter. The only person whose opinion should matter is you.

10

SUCCESS IS LOOKING FOR YOU

"There is something special inside each one of us that gives us permission to succeed."

The level of success that you desire is waiting on you to reach out and grab it. Now that you have read through the process outlined in the previous chapters and taken extensive notes, it is time for you to take massive action toward achieving success.

In grade school, I was assigned a science project that included watching a caterpillar evolve into a butterfly, a process, I learned, that is called metamorphosis. Plainly speaking, metamorphosis is the process of transforming from one state of existence to the next. It's a word often used synonymously with positive change and growth.

The objective for my project was to observe and record the four metamorphic stages from larva to butterfly. In its infant or immature stage, I found the larva or caterpillar to be slimy and grossly unattractive. Once the caterpillar matures it forms a shell around itself called a pupa. During the pupa stage, the caterpillar slowly transitions into an adult butterfly that eventually emerges fully formed from its green cocoon and into the world.

Each of our lives can be viewed like this, as a series of stages through which we must pass and transform. Each of us is a work in progress and every stage has its purpose. Every stage, whether exultant or arduous, plays a major role in building our character and delivering us to our destiny. Seeking success can be an overwhelming experience. You may be tempted to give up. If you hit a roadblock, simply find another route around what prohibits your success.

Fear and doubt must never be an option. When overcome with thoughts of past and future failure, when worried by impeded progress, remember the parable of the fig tree. Luke 13:6-9 tells of a man who plants a fig tree in his vineyard. One day the man checks on the fig tree and discovers the fig tree is bare. With much disappointment he tells his gardener to cut down the tree. After three years, the tree had yet to bear fruit, the man says. The tree is using up precious soil. The gardener, in response, begs the man to give the fig tree one more year. The gardener promises to cultivate and tend the tree and pledges to surely cut it down if it fails to bear fruit the next year. This parable is a clear example of how the gardener believed in the fig tree and never gave up on the possibility of the tree bearing fruit.

In this parable think of God as the owner, Christ as the gardener, and ourselves as the fig tree. When we were barren of fruit, when we failed to embody our own and best true nature, Christ interceded on our behalf and took us under his nurturing care. He did not give up on us, just as we must not give up on ourselves.

In John 15:4 Christ said, "Abide in me, and I in you. As a branch cannot bear fruit by itself, unless it abides in the vine neither can you, unless you abide in me."

Christ, as our gardener, believes in our innate capacity to flourish and grow and offers His guiding hand. He grants you permission to shine. We spend a great deal of time and energy seeking that which is already inside us. Each of us is blessed with talents and abilities, special and unique. Take the time to develop your *why*, visualize your success, prepare yourself for change, and stay the course. Remember, you are your own best asset. You have permission to succeed.

VISUALIZING YOUR SUCCESS: CREATING A VISION BOARD

In order for you to achieve the goals that you have set, you must have a clear vision of your desired success and the end result. As stated earlier on this chapter, **"Visualizing Your Success"** includes living it every day and dreaming of success every night."

A highly effective way to visualize your goals is to create a visual reference for your goals. There is no right or wrong way to create a visual reference. Some people write their goals on a sticky note and post in on their mirror. Posting your goals on your mirror will force you to look at those goals every time you look in the mirror. Some people post notes of encouragement on the refrigerator or on the back of the door that they exit before leaving their home. There are various methods used for creating a visual reference. The most creative and effective tool is a "Vision Board."

A [3]vision board is a collage of pictures and words usually made from sturdy poster board, cork board or materials used for

---

[3] The sample "vision board" was used as a reference from the website http://www.catalogofdreams.com/images/visionboard

presentations or displays. Simply find articles, words and pictures that inspire you and post them on the board. Find pictures of your desired house, car, lifestyle, vacation destinations, etc. When visualizing your success one of your goals should always be to remain rooted in God's word and the path that he has for you. Be sure to incorporate your desire for spiritual growth when creating your vision board. Creating a vision board will help you stay focused and steadfast in achieving your goals. When visualizing your success you should visualize your desired success from conception to birth. By creating a vision board you are surrounding yourself with images that will become a part of you. Each time you look at your vision board the images will become imbedded in your mind and become a part of you forcing you to worker harder to achieve success.

To some this idea may sound juvenile or time consuming, but if you can see it then you can achieve it! Think of your vision board as a mule thinks of chasing a carrot tied to the end of a stick. There is a popular anecdote that tells the story of a mule chasing a carrot. According to this old adage, a few decades ago when farmers used mules for plowing, they would tie a carrot to the end of a stick and hold the stick in front of a mule. The carrot served as motivation for the mule to plow the field and aide in producing a prosperous crop for the farmer. As long as the mule could visualize the carrot he had something to work toward, he had a goal! Just as the mule worked hard because he could see his end result you should clearly see your end result and work hard toward attaining your goal.

VISUALIZE YOUR SUCCESS - LIST YOUR IDEA OF WHAT WILL MAKE YOU SUCCESSFUL

Let us begin by clearly defining the word vision in the context that I address throughout "You Have Permission to Succeed." When we hear the word *vision* we often think of something supernatural or some sort of ocular abstraction that seems ambiguous. Some of us have visions that include becoming more successful, obtaining wealth, getting a husband/wife but we think in vague terms. When visualizing your desired success, you should always stretch your vision to the limit. Develop a well-defined in-depth vision that will enable you to see beyond the surface and penetrate deep into your mind.

1. What is your definition of success?

_____

_____

_____

_____

_____

_____

2. List and clearly define your vision for success in each area.

Vision: Business/Career

_____

_____

_____

_____

_____

_____

Personal Growth:

_____

_____

_____

_____

_____

_____

Relationships (marriage, dating, friendships, professional)

_____

_____

_____

_____

_____

_____

Finances:

_____

_____

_____

_____

_____

Spiritual Growth:

_____

_____

_____

_____

_____

Family:

_____

_____

_____

_____

Happiness:

_____

_____

_____

_____

_____

_____

List and define your vision for success in a category that was not mentioned above

_____

_____

_____

_____

_____

_____

Prioritize your attributes of success

1. _____

2. _____

3. _____

4. _____

5. _____

6. _____

7. _____

After prioritizing your vision, address them in the order of priority as listed below. Please refer to Chapter 3, "Set Specific Goals" to assist in properly assessing your short term and long terms goals.

My Vision: _____

Elements of your vision:

Goal: What is your specific goal for your vision?

Short Term Goal:

✓ _____
   _____
   _____
   _____

Completion Date: _____

Long Term Goal:

✓ _____
   _____
   _____
   _____

Completion Date: _____

Strengths: What are the positive aspects that you currently posses that will assist you in obtaining this goal and why are?

✓ _____

_____

_____

_____

✓ _____

_____

_____

_____

Obstacles: What obstacles do you feel will hinder you from obtaining your goal?

✓ _____

_____

_____

_____

✓ _____

_____

_____

_____

Action: What steps will I take to make my vision a reality?

✓ _____

_____

_____

_____

✓ _____

_____

_____

_____

✓ _____

_____

_____

_____

My Vision: _____

Elements of your vision:

Goal: What is your specific goal for your vision?

Short Term Goal:

✓ _____
_____
_____
_____

Completion Date: _____

Long Term Goal:

✓ _____
_____
_____
_____

Completion Date: _____

Strengths: What are the positive aspects that you currently posses that will assist you in obtaining this goal and why are?

✓ _____
_____
_____
_____

✓ _____
_____
_____
_____

Obstacles: What obstacles do you feel will hinder you from obtaining your goal?

✓ _____
_____
_____
_____

✓ _____
_____
_____
_____

Action: What steps will I take to make my vision a reality?

✓ _____
_____
_____
_____

✓ _____
_____
_____
_____

✓ _____
_____
_____
_____

My Vision: _____

Elements of your vision:

Goal: What is your specific goal for your vision?

Short Term Goal:

✓ _____
_____
_____
_____

Completion Date: _____

Long Term Goal:

✓ _____
_____
_____
_____

Completion Date: _____

Strengths: What are the positive aspects that you currently posses that will assist you in obtaining this goal and why are?

✓ _____

_____

_____

_____

✓ _____

_____

_____

_____

Obstacles: What obstacles do you feel will hinder you from obtaining your goal?

✓ _____

_____

_____

_____

✓ _____

_____

_____

_____

Action: What steps will I take to make my vision a reality?

✓ _____

_____

_____

_____

✓ _____

_____

_____

_____

✓ _____

_____

_____

_____

My Vision: _____

Elements of your vision:

Goal: What is your specific goal for your vision?

Short Term Goal:

✓ _____
_____
_____
_____

Completion Date: _____

Long Term Goal:

✓ _____
_____
_____
_____

Completion Date: _____

Strengths: What are the positive aspects that you currently posses that will assist you in obtaining this goal and why are?

✓ _____

   _____

   _____

   _____

✓ _____

   _____

   _____

   _____

Obstacles: What obstacles do you feel will hinder you from obtaining your goal?

✓ _____

   _____

   _____

   _____

✓ _____

   _____

   _____

   _____

Action: What steps will I take to make my vision a reality?

✓ _____
_____
_____
_____

✓ _____
_____
_____
_____

✓ _____
_____
_____
_____

My Vision: _____

Elements of your vision:

Goal: What is your specific goal for your vision?

Short Term Goal:

✓ _____

_____

_____

_____

Completion Date: _____

Long Term Goal:

✓ _____

_____

_____

_____

Completion Date: _____

Strengths: What are the positive aspects that you currently posses that will assist you in obtaining this goal and why are?

✓ _____
_____
_____
_____

✓ _____
_____
_____
_____

Obstacles: What obstacles do you feel will hinder you from obtaining your goal?

✓ _____
_____
_____
_____

✓ _____
_____
_____
_____

Action: What steps will I take to make my vision a reality?

✓ _____
   _____
   _____
   _____

✓ _____
   _____
   _____
   _____

✓ _____
   _____
   _____
   _____

My Vision: _____

Elements of your vision:

Goal: What is your specific goal for your vision?

Short Term Goal:

✓ _____
_____
_____
_____

Completion Date: _____

Long Term Goal:

✓ _____
_____
_____
_____

Completion Date: _____

Strengths: What are the positive aspects that you currently posses that will assist you in obtaining this goal and why are?

✓ _____

_____

_____

_____

✓ _____

_____

_____

_____

Obstacles: What obstacles do you feel will hinder you from obtaining your goal?

✓ _____

_____

_____

_____

✓ _____

_____

_____

_____

Action: What steps will I take to make my vision a reality?

✓ _____
_____
_____
_____

✓ _____
_____
_____
_____

✓ _____
_____
_____
_____

My Vision: _____

Elements of your vision:

Goal: What is your specific goal for your vision?

Short Term Goal:

✓ _____
_____
_____
_____

Completion Date: _____

Long Term Goal:

✓ _____
_____
_____
_____

Completion Date: _____

Strengths: What are the positive aspects that you currently posses that will assist you in obtaining this goal and why are?

✓ _____
_____
_____
_____

✓ _____
_____
_____
_____

Obstacles: What obstacles do you feel will hinder you from obtaining your goal?

✓ _____
_____
_____
_____

✓ _____
_____
_____
_____

Action: What steps will I take to make my vision a reality?

✓ _____
_____
_____
_____

✓ _____
_____
_____
_____

✓ _____
_____
_____
_____

Identify the Things That You Need to Change
(Include your name and why you need to change)

I _____ will change:

_____
_____
_____
_____

I _____ will change:

_____
_____
_____
_____

I _____ will change:

_____
_____
_____
_____

I _____ will change:

_____
_____
_____
_____

I _____ will change:

_____
_____
_____
_____

I _____ **will change:**

_____
_____
_____
_____

INDENTIFY YOUR BIGGEST FEARS OR INSECURITIES THAT MAY HINDER YOUR PROGRESS

FEAR #1

_____

_____

_____

_____

FEAR #2

_____

_____

_____

_____

FEAR #3

_____

_____

_____

_____

WORKS CITED

Alessandra, Tony, Janice Van Dyke and Michael J. O'Connor. People Smarts: Bending the Golden Rule to Give Others What They Want. Pfeiffer & Co, 1994.

Cunningham, Sean. "Ten Best Mothers Ever." Esquire 7 May 2009: 2.

Hill, Napoleon. The Master Key to Riches. Fawcett Publications, Inc, 1965.

—. Think and Grow Rich. Forgotten Books, 2008.

Hughes, Langston. "A Drean Deferred." Hughes, Langston, Arnold Rampersad and David Roessel. The Collected Poems of Langston Hughes. New Jersey: Vintage; 1st Vintage Classics Ed edition, 1995. 426.

Maxwell, John C. Develop The Leader Within You. Nashville: Thomas Nelson, LLC., Publishing, 2000.

Widener, Chrus. The Angel Inside. Yoursuccessstore.com, 2007.

SUGGESTED READING

Alessandra, Tony, Janice Van Dyke and Michael J. O'Connor. People Smarts: Bending the Golden Rule to Give Others What They Want. Pfeiffer & Co, 1994.

Carnegie, Dale. How to Win Friends and Influence People. Simon and Schuster, 2009

Clason, George S. The Richest Man in Babylon, Signit, 2004

Hill, Napoleon. Think and Grow Rich. Forgotten Books, 2008.

Hill, Napoleon. The Master Key to Riches. Fawcett Publications, Inc, 1965.

Kiyosaki, Robert. Rich Dad Poor Dad. New York: Warner Books, 1997

Kiyosaki, Robert. Rich Dad's Increase Your Financial IQ: It's Time to Get Smarter with Your Money. Grand Central Publishing, 2009

Maxwell, John C. Developing the Leaders Around You: How to Help Others Reach Their Full Potential. Nelson Business, 2005

Maxwell, John C. 21 Irrefutable Laws of Leadership. Nashville: Thomas Nelson, INC. 2007

ABOUT THE AUTHOR

As a motivational speaker, successful businessman and author, Edwin Haynes continues to dominate his industry as a multimillionaire while empowering individuals worldwide to advance on both personal and professional levels. As a Trainer and International Business Consultant, he continues to make an indelible impression on those he encounters daily. In an effort to satisfy an overwhelming demand for his knowledge and plan for success, Edwin has penned the first installment of a planned series of motivational publications entitled *"You Have Permission to Succeed."*

In this work, Haynes takes the reader on a journey to emotional, economic and spiritual prosperity. His goal is to help the reader to effectively navigate his or her way through internal and external obstacles, inducing their place on the road to success. Edwin encourages the readers to manifest their desires by setting specific goals and mastering effective leadership. Holding true to the belief that success is only a decision away, Edwin Haynes delivers a guide to life that will motivate readers to be masters of success leading only to infinite destiny.

Blessed with the gift of captivating audiences with his seemingly effortless yet down-to-earth and honest style, Haynes changes the lives of thousands weekly through consistent messages of faith, encouragement and empowerment.

After a successful thirteen-year career as an Entertainment Executive, Haynes transitioned into a career as a Success Coach achieving unprecedented success immediately. Currently, he is one of the top income earners for the world's largest healthy coffee distributor and has fostered one of the company's fastest growing teams. As a result of his staunch dedication, generosity and genuine good nature, Haynes was awarded his previous company's esteemed 2004 "Going the Extra Mile" award as well as, in 2006, its most prestigious "Man of the Year" award.

Inspiring a team of over 30,000 general members and over 150,000 independent business owners, Haynes is recognized as one of the company's premier trainers and presenters. When asked to give advice for someone just venturing into the realm of entrepreneurship, he offered these memorable words "Hook your wagon to a star…proper mentorship is to successful networking what air is to life…you can't have one without the other."

Edwin Haynes has developed comprehensive personal and professional enrichment programs that are tailored to the client's needs. Edwin is committed to sharing life changing knowledge with clients from all walks of life whether it's one or a group of several hundred. As a speaker, Edwin Haynes delivers a dynamic message based on nine key principles that will guide you on your road to success. To book Edwin Haynes for Speaking Engagements, Corporate Training, Leadership Training, Team Building and/or Personal Enrichment Coaching, please contact E. Haynes Publishing, LLC.

Thank you for your continued support. Remember you are your best asset and you have permission to succeed!

E. Haynes Publishing. LLC
2470 S. Dairy Ashford, Suite 217
Houston, TX 77077
Phone: 713-493-0566
Email: ehaynes@ehaynespublishing.com
www.edwinhaynes.com